I'LL BELIEVE *that* THE DAY I SEE YOU FLY!

:SORRY:

I CAN'T HEAR YOU

OVER THE

volume

OF MY HAIR

KNITWEAR: soooooo UNDERRATED.

I'M GETTING REALLY SICK AND *tired* OF FOOD HAVING CALORIES

Burp!

TOUGH DAY
AT THE OFFICE...

PAPERWORK
PILED
UP!

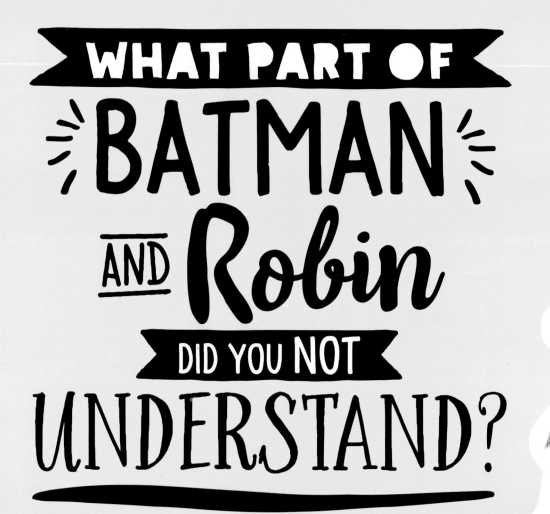

:BOYS:

WILL NEVER UNDERSTAND THE

STRUGGLE

OF LONG HAIR

AND

lipstick

ON A WINDY DAY

YOGA AT HOME...

HARDER THAN YOU THINK

THE AWKWARD

STEP-SIBLING

photo shoot...

#HUGITOUT

#OMG!

I'VE SEEN THINGS
I JUST
WASN'T
MEANT TO SEE

RIGHT, EMPTY YOUR POCKETS *again.*

I KNOW SOMEONE'S GOT MY KEYS.

#GUILTYLOOKING

IF ONLY YOU WERE AS

fabulous

AS,

oh I DON'T KNOW,

me!

CAN SOMEONE

PLEASE TELL ME WHEN

MONDAY'S

OVER

Oh, THE IRONY.